T0158112

Looking Glass

Contemplating Philosophies of Real Life

Marissa Madrid

iUniverse, Inc.
New York   Bloomington

Looking Glass
Contemplating Philosophies of Real Life

Copyright © Marissa Madrid

All rights reserved. No part of this book may be used or reproduced by any means, graphic, electronic, or mechanical, including photocopying, recording, taping or by any information storage retrieval system without the written permission of the publisher except in the case of brief quotations embodied in critical articles and reviews.

The views expressed in this work are solely those of the author and do not necessarily reflect the views of the publisher, and the publisher hereby disclaims any responsibility for them.

iUniverse books may be ordered through booksellers or by contacting:

iUniverse
1663 Liberty Drive
Bloomington, IN 47403
www.iuniverse.com
1-800-Authors (1-800-288-4677)

Because of the dynamic nature of the Internet, any Web addresses or links contained in this book may have changed since publication and may no longer be valid. The views expressed in this work are solely those of the author and do not necessarily reflect the views of the publisher, and the publisher hereby disclaims any responsibility for them.

ISBN: 978-1-4401-1500-4 (pbk)
ISBN: 978-1-4401-1502-8 (ebk)

Library of Congress Control Number: 2008944247

Printed in the United States of America

iUniverse rev. date: 12/29/2008

Preface

In the Fall Semester of 2008, I was invited to participate as a virtual guest at a Chicago college in three classes (2 Social Science and 1 African American Studies), via my internet blogs. As an advocate and liaison in my community who organizes partnerships and programs, I accepted the invitation with a vision to connect educators and students through modern methods of communication and the potential to bridge gaps between all ages and cultures within educational structures.

As demonstrated through comments which students left on the three internet blogs, the supplemental material was inviting and provided an opportunity to observe how educators may continue to utilize such technology to improve and broaden the range of learned concepts. Students who posted their comments and feedback appeared to be engaged and acquired a more meaningful grasp of lessons in the writings; along with my efforts to nurture students with encouragement, thought provoking challenges, and healthy views of the world.

I now reflect on what made the blogs appealing and result in positive outcomes-concluding there is a strategy. A crucial element of implementing and embedding the blogs into a curriculum is personalizing the shared information. People want something real, inspirational, and mind stimulating to make them feel good deep down inside... something they can relate to. Dedicated educators and writers walk the same path of capturing the attention of their audience through quality literature and innovative means to teach. They pay attention to what works with the better interest of all in mind-for the sake of achievement in and out of the class room. If we look to the history of all people, education begins within family and community; and their lessons taught through stories stretch into our modern time. It is a wonderful period to be a student and instructor with not only traditional text books and lectures, but also with the ability to learn directly from the source of other societies; carrying on traditions of education and rich culture half way around the world, with infinite information in all forms of media.

As I review comments posted to the blogs, it is easy to map what led students to become engaged and how it impacted their thoughts, writing, and confidence/comfort level of sharing knowledge and thought. To promote independent thoughts and views I included personal stories, poetry, and philosophy-challenging individuals to think in addition to and beyond what they have read in the required texts. This approach was readily discovered upon my reading of the instructor's syllabus to develop the customized blogs; naturally blending into the scope of desired goals of what was to be taught. Just as writing and teaching is art, so is learning which calls upon extensions of materials. It demands asking open ended questions, provisions of stories and examples to inspire how the student identifies his/herself with the assigned lessons, and a moderator to maintain a safe online environment where all participants have a voice followed with praise and even more information based on their responses. In addition to the personal writings, I included valuable related links for all to explore and obtain extensive information.

The following is the undeniable impact of the blogs witnessed within student's feedback:

- A student's comment was posted in Spanish and the communication was made available to all through means of translation resources (respect for one's culture and opportunity for others to learn from)

- Students posted comments, personally identifying with the subject, issue, and challenge (providing the instructor with another form of assessing abilities in comprehension and contribution)

- Students initiating class room discussions with blog information as the foundation (an opportunity for the instructor to merge online material with texts)

- A student left comments and requests for further reading of the like from the author (demonstrates continuing desire for reading and knowledge)

- Comments of appreciation for another resource to make the class more interesting have been left (a tool for motivation and inspiration to write not mechanically, but meaningfully)

These five details are only but a few of the endless benefits to educators who find alternative, creative, and modern evolving methods to teaching. As the author and creator of the proven blogs, I anticipate and embrace future partnering with more educators in similar endeavors and vision of providing quality, professional, and dedicated learning to those who reach for higher education with real life skills. I express gratitude to the professor of these classes who included my work as part of the priceless education Olive-Harvey College prides in its students, as part of a most rewarding collaboration.

Foreword

As the Director of West Center for Intergenerational Learning and during the years of working with Community Liaison, Marissa Madrid, she has consistently proven a high level of dedication to educating and advocating for our community of all ages. Marissa is an individual of extreme creativity and inspires others to expand their minds while forming partnerships to serve and better neighborhoods, non-profit and educational establishments. Her readers are challenged to think deeper and to speculate their significance to society and the environment. Marissa is on a set path to empower others, as she assists them with integral talent found in her vision, literature, and actions.

The compilations of original internet blogs Marissa included in this published work, has a personable and awakening take compared to traditional views. The blogs consist of writings, designed to blend into a curriculum for college students for extras in learning. She used a concise approach to gaining the readers' attention; and follows their comments with a mentor, perhaps even *maternal* like disposition. The response left from the college students attests to Marissa's intention to stimulate independent thinking and reaching out to others over all distances by implementing our fast growing opportunities found on the internet. Local readers and followers of her writing have testified to positive emotions and motivation drawn from Marissa's timeless memoirs, poetry, and philosophical pieces. A sharp and ambitious humanitarian author for sure... and a valuable asset to all who experience Marissa's messages of compassion, love, and good will through her writing, photography, art, and all inclusive services.

E.D. Rucker
City of Colorado Springs
Parks, Recreation, & Cultural Services

Acknowledgements

I express endless gratitude to my colleagues, students, and all who genuinely share their beautiful views of life with me; only to further what I imagine us as learning from and growing together in effort to create a place of unity between educators, scholars, and those who are passionate about the future of our youth-as we lead them by example.

Introduction

The layout of Looking Glass was designed with the ability to view the literature, resources, and comments (only a few select due to the abundance) similarly to what is viewed online. All of the memoirs are based on true life experiences and the other pieces are derived from a quiet place of contemplating symbolic measures of life and what it holds in past, present, and future for human kind. The first blog is titled the same as this book, Looking Glass. The second blog, Spectrums was utilized along with the first for two Social Science classes. The third is Sankofa and was imbedded within the African American Studies syllabus. The experience of watching the blogs cultivate with views of the students has been most rewarding and encouraging to resume with adding more seeds to this educational substratum.

Looking Glass-Blog I

I AM

Many see me as beauty.
That's not me.
I am a single source of energy waiting to touch the world.
Like a bird soaring high to capture grace.
That of a growing tree branching importance to everyone's life.
A given flower in return for simple happiness.
Stars seen to remind one of existence.
Warmth from fire to comfort a soul.
A spirit that remembers to remain humble.
A child who is in motion as the earth spins and a new universe is
born.
It is not what I am; only that I am.

copy right 2008 Life Mind

Reflecting on all of the things we are perceived as by others-isn't half as important as knowing why we are here, determined by the free will of individual choice.

"I AM" is an insightful, powerful, well articulated reflective narrative. I had to read it a few times to come to a fuller appreciation of the interplay and tension found in the use of its words. I found easement in the methodic utilization and arrangement of your use of words and language, to resolve these symbols called letters/alphabets into a reflective unity of being. It was more of an ontological transformation, into another realm in sharing the inner core, of your inner-self with others. Excellent writing.

Gustavus

SEPTEMBER 19, 2008 7:37 AM

TiMe

This thing to measure our existence and how we apply it is most interesting. Too soon, passes too fast, running out of it, and perhaps wasted. If a thousand years on earth equates one second in the heavens, why not create our own frame together where it's ok to freely use it in a passive more appreciative way? "They married too soon." or "He wasted all that time." Who's to say that the generalization applies to each or all individuals? How much is too much spent? I say trust your gut and recognize the pivoting moment when you believe 100% in a vision... when you feel the pure emotion of love and passion for your life's work or maybe even another person. And, when you know that regardless of all who doubt, your dream to make your life more important than you alone is a must go full throttle. Doubt is based on fear of those who complied with social acceptance of commonality in not being worthy of living the fullest life possible. "Full", meaning enjoying each moment with conviction and purpose. Forget testing the waters and make some waves! Just some thoughts dedicated to those who discourage, doubt, and attempt to crush great dreamers of yesterday, today, and tomorrow. I also suggest they inhale the dust left behind from the moment I chose to ignore their ignorance and move forward.

Through Weather and Time Leadville, CO copy right 2006

Time is the coin of your life. It is the only coin you have, and only you can determine how it will be spent. Be careful lest you let other people spend it for you.
~Carl Sandburg

This blog on time reminds me to not feel that whatever I have done was not a waste of time, but was time well spent for a purpose of whatever I was trying to accomplish at that period in life.

Shareese

SEPTEMBER 5, 2008 12:48 PM

The "Time" blog is a very important material in life. I just realized how important time is in life. I was basically raised in two different cultures one in which time wasn't really considered important, being on time was just moving on a slow pace. The other culture was the opposite; time is considered as everything, being on time can illustrate a lot about you. It is viewed as a path to success.

Latoya

SEPTEMBER 6, 2008 12:17 PM

The most significant saying that stood out was "Doubt is based on fear of those who complied with social acceptance of commonality". I truly believe that 100 percent. Mediocrity Hates Excellence, plain and simple, and it will do everything in its power to drag everyone and everything down to its level. If one truly wishes to surpass his\her own goals (not society preplanned/preapproved goals), then they must defeat their own worst enemies; fear and our own selves.

Anthony

SEPTEMBER 7, 2008 8:20 AM

I love the wonderful and empowering feedback you all have left. An important question I feel that applies to the concept of "time" and "acceptance" is "Are the results of your efforts worthy of you?"

Periodically I like to share recommended readings to extend/expand on messages I attempt to convey. Perhaps some of you would enjoy this:

"The human will, that force unseen,
The offspring of a deathless soul,
Can hew away any goal,

Though walls of granite intervene."
James Allen, As a Man Thinketh

Thanks to all of you and please continue to share as it suits you.

Kind regards,
Marissa

SEPTEMBER 8, 2008 9:49 AM

I found this reading on time very interesting. I agreed with the message in the reading. The part that I mainly liked was... "I say trust your gut and recognize the pivoting moment when you believe 100% in a vision...when you feel the pure emotion of love and passion for your life's work or maybe even another person. And, when you know that regardless of all who doubt, your dream to make your life more important than you alone is a must go full throttle." This caught my attention because many doubt my success in life. I am here to prove them wrong. I'm striving for this dream with everything I have.

Rio

SEPTEMBER 8, 2008 11:48 PM

Marissa,

It's funny how a person can step out and search for something better in life and they find kind words like these looking back at them when they least expect it. So funny how these particular words are the exact beginnings from where I come from; the exact struggles that I am facing today. At times like these, and words like that are what I truly feel are words from the heavens sent to the person that has the courage to say them in the midst so much negativity. Thank you so much for being that person. Always remember that out of the abundance of the heart, so shall you speak. And when you speak out positive things like this, you are giving people the words that they've needed to hear, inspiring them to do what they've been waiting for so long to do. Words like these are much more than words when spoken from an outpour of emotions, feelings, and thoughts... they are golden secrets from an Angel being whispered into the ears of those who cry out at night for yearnings of a better tomorrow.

Ash

SEPTEMBER 9, 2008 8:55 AM

Marissa;despues de haber leido el blog me doy cuenta de algunas similitudes hacia tu interpretacion sobre el tiempo. Tiempo es valioso para tu vida, no importa si lo supiste o no aprovechar, lo importante es que ese tiempo dedicado te ha dado experiencia y por lo cual as adquirido mas pasajes a tu vida.Sin embargo es bueno darle el mejor uso posible.

Silvia

SEPTEMBER 12, 2008 3:23 PM

For the sake of remaining ALL inclusive and considerate to all readers...if you are curious/interested in discovering the translation between us two, go to the following link:

http://translation2.paralink.com/

(copy and paste the content)

Silvia~
Gracias por las palabras de sabiduría.
Marissa

SEPTEMBER 12, 2008 4:02 PM

The earliest recorded African philosophy of time was expounded by the ancient Egyptian thinker Ptahhotep (c. 2650–2600 BC), who said: "Do not lessen the time of following desire, for the wasting of time is an abomination to the spirit."[citation needed] The Vedas, the earliest texts on Indian philosophy and Hindu philosophy dating back to the late 2nd millennium BC, describe ancient Hindu cosmology, in which the universe goes through repeated cycles of creation, destruction and rebirth, with each cycle lasting 4,320,000 years. Ancient Greek philosophers, including Parmenides and Heraclitus, wrote essays on the nature of time.[21]

In Book 11 of St. Augustine's Confessions, he ruminates on the nature of time, asking, "What then is time? If no one asks me, I know: if I wish to explain it to one that asketh, I know not." He settles on time being defined more by what it is not than what it is.[22]

Gustavus

SEPTEMBER 22, 2008 6:05 AM

Marissa, in her comments, tries to show the importance of time, and how to apply it in a profitable way. She sees time as something that measures our existence, and also as a vehicle that travels with us. She expresses that sometimes it's ahead of us, together with us some other times, and still at times behind us. Everything we do, should be the result of our evaluation of what the priority of the moment is. I think she is right, and I praise her understanding of time. Everyone should take his or her distance to examine when and when not to do something, what to and what not to do, how to and how not to do whatever they have decided to do. However, I do not picture time only as the measure of my existence; I prefer to propose that I measure my existence through a gage I call time. For me, time is eternal; it does not go anywhere. I am the vehicle in motion; time is just the road. I just need to control my speed, my stops, and my choices on the road. I pass and go, but time remains the same. When nature and everything that is in the universe grow old, we think time grows old, too. But it doesn't. The one that lives eternally always uses time in the present because for him, there is no past and no future. He promises that those who trust him will grow in nature, and will be able to picture time as an eternal present when this universe, as we know it, grows old and passes away. All considerations Marissa made are interesting and valuable but not because time is passing by, but because we are passing by in time, and won't be around to make up for what we failed doing in our life.

SEPTEMBER 22, 2008 6:38 AM

Spectrums-Blog II

Choices

Scenario:

A man enters a convenience store to steal a pack of batteries. The cashier, a young man, witnesses the crime in progress. As the thief bolts toward the door, the cashier runs after him and out the door. The pursuit heads into a busy street where the thief escapes and the cashier is fatally injured by a car.

Results:

Do you think only the two men are affected by the event? If so, think again.

The cashier has a brother in Iraq, fighting with other soldiers in the war. The cashier helps take care of his brother's family monetarily and by watching his niece and nephew after school, so their mother can contribute to the household. Imagine the anguish they all experience knowing that their brother didn't have to fight in the war to die.

The thief on the other hand, was apprehended thanks to surveillance cameras. This is another add on to his record and he is sent back to prison... leaving his girlfriend to fend for their children financially, emotionally, and physically. Their eldest son finds a hint of glory in dad's "rough and tough" life style. By the age of 14, the boy is in juvenile jail-off to a steady beginning of having a life term criminal profession. His two siblings often take five minutes of attention per day from mom- as she has to appear in court for brother, work 2 jobs, and take naps where possible.

Moral of the story:

Many of us fail to realize exactly how important of a role we play in society, and the environment. We turn a blind eye, claim we can't afford to pay attention, and a wide range of other excuses to avoid small contributions or our ability to lead others by example. In no way do I suggest we make choices that only please others but, do make choices which never attach our names to anything harmful to each other, or ourselves. We are all intrinsic beings in this world- and thinking that each living thing is independent of our existence is a downfall in any community or society. Let's make good choices so no one can take the right to do so away. Success breeds success...be good to each other!

Linked

Look to the mountains and ask "why?" See the eyes of our children and ask "how do we teach them that our resources are not infinite?"

What was once Aspens, Pines, and tall grass is now a deep scar. From the wound, dust is blown as a visual scream of the great mounds. Years carry the healing process of a range struggling to remain in existence.

The wealthy come crashing in with homes large enough for five families and displace wild life; providing work for the minimally paid builders. These high rollers pave a dark road to the clearing where the house is erected-and this is what they call *appreciation* for the great out doors.

The animals migrate to the city where they are confused and lost; leading to attacks on people and their pets, though it is they who are filled with fear. They haven't a domain to return to for the *appreciation* claimed it.

The rivers and creeks flow low in addition to drought while greens turn to brown and yellow. Climate changes, natural disasters increase, and what causes it all does not change.

Solution?

- Demonstrate for future generations, that having children is not a novelty.

- Live in homes which already exist and do not destroy those of others

- Emphasize how we are all linked and follow the old Native American proverb:

We do not inherit the earth from our ancestors; we borrow it from our children.

Tree-o-Solo Gold Camp Road, CO copy right 2006

We as humans destroy in order to live, un-instinctively. We live off others misfortune and move them from there natural habitats. We hate naturalists and adore what man makes of us. Barely embracing what it means to enjoy the simpler god given wonders and idolizing man made toxins.

A.C.

SEPTEMBER 4, 2008 11:21 AM

Well expressed! But, what do you feel is each individual's responsibility to improve such a dismal state of our society? I often witness others making the same observations...only to be ignored for lack of ambition and desire to make a change. Thanks for sharing!

Marissa

SEPTEMBER 5, 2008 9:26 AM

Cry of the Child

Some where before your eyes, is a growing child. The four year old appears to play, be curious, and sing like the others. You note his laughter, smiles, and nature to be joyful. Over a period of time you begin to notice his eyes tend to drift into a distance. In making the observation as a new piece, you wonder if he is daydreaming of far off places, a moment when Mom comes to pick him up, or other happy instances. The boy's expression is blank. What can this new mind hold? He can't tell anyone he's abused, scared, and alone at home.

Some months down the road your little friend develops new methods to stir his amusement followed with smiles and laughter. Along with his actions, comes the crying of his peers, at various times. Chairs sometimes hit the floor. Toys find their way into his bag if they survive attempts of destruction. Adults make effort to redirect the behavior and, he simply smiles in defiance. His pain begins to manifest in the world before his eyes.

A few years down the path the boy discovers amateur weapons and how powerful he feels when using them to intimidate others. Neighbors notice the louder, harsher music…holes in the yard and walls of the house, and disassembled toys strung through out. Teachers witness his gradual descent in grades and withdraw from others. He waits for rescue. He wants to be free. No pain. No more abuse to him…or his pain… he will project onto others.

He grows in years and so do the injuries. He no longer sheds tears. He is numb.

Imagine now, the following potential tragedies to endure:

His surrounding society ignores his obvious demise by abuse. No one says a word, other than harsh judgments toward his unusual and questionable behavior. The final injury is fatal.

or

He runs away to feel accepted. And, he feels belonging with the exploitation of his very being.

or

He feels no one will ever know his pain unless he shares and imposes it. With revenge in his heart, he destroys others.

How can we choose to continue evading the cry of a child knowing the ramifications? How can we as society point at the children who suffer not only their position, but also our judgment? When their voice is muffled and nothing is left to communicate with but acting out, who will hear the cry of the child?

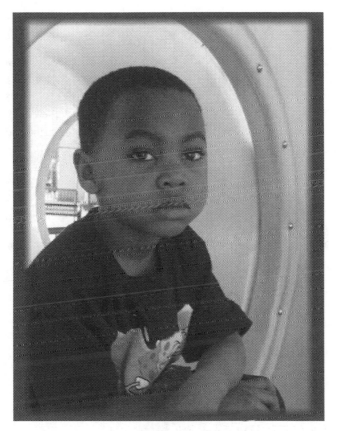

Serious copy right 2005

We are guilty of ignoring the saying, "It takes a village to raise a child". This is an example of the importance of that saying. We are blessed with five senses but don't take advantage of them to save a child. It can be as simple as love.

Chiquita

SEPTEMBER 24, 2008 9:24 AM

I've never understood how people can just simply bypass a child's cries. I mean, it's not a meaningless sound check on a microphone at your local spoken word set. No matter how big or small the problem is, there's a problem. This is my whole motivation to become a child psychologist. I mean, I'd like to think that people are ignorant to the fact that children have issues as well and they're even more vulnerable to these issues because they're nothing more than children. They have almost no independent resources. I think children often act out as the four year old Marissa wrote about because it's one of the most primitive forms of expression. Violence towards his toys, other inanimate objects, and peers is the best way the child knows to express to the world that something's not right.

Al

SEPTEMBER 18, 2008 9:27 PM

As an educator I can stress the importance of being an advocate for children. Often times, I have come to the rescue of children in need. Their silent cry was my call for action! Many years ago it became my mission to provide support to these children and their families. It is important for everyone to help—these children are our future parents and leaders. I've often wondered how one can turn their backs on children when they can see the look of longing in their eyes--the look of helplessness, the look of wonder. I wonder if one could turn a blind eye if they had a crystal ball to look into the future. If they could see the damage neglect can cause. Maybe we should all think about the future— our future leaders, future parents, future advocates.

Patricia Johnson

SEPTEMBER 23, 2008 3:34 PM

Not Webster Defined

Based on one woman's personal experience, she defines the following:

Genius-Is an individual who recognizes each natural phenomenal occurrence; with innate curiosity and ambition to discover the function and purpose of all existence. And, how humanity effects and/or has the ability to change or contribute to the inner twining birth of every evolutionary phase that has been and will be within the universe. The genius believes in no limits except for what is projected by the mind. He or she simply does with minimal regard for risk; due to over abundance of passion in a cause or vision.

Brilliance-Falls not far from genius with the additional, apparent appeal of creations and ideas that call to the spirit of others. Genius exists among good and bad; for the cause of destruction and invention alike. Genius with brilliance combined sets forth more illuminating results of a masterful individual not to be torn between influences of outside motives, selfishness, and/or greed.

Intent-Germinates within every genius...for without intent there is no ambition which determines the high level of commitment to the final result of one's life work. Positive energy and intent are more readily recognized with brilliance; leading the individual to self efficacy-opposed to those who for more negative causes never achieve.

Love~Is the vessel of all great things to come, learn from, and to experience. No living thing could be created without love by its creator; demonstrated in the thought, time, patience, and determination to pour such masses of the self into it. Love is any thing we passionately with good will devote ourselves to with an unconditional acceptance of what can or could be. As the receivers of love, we observe and recognize a deep penetrating unspoken language through the soul of the eyes and through an inexplicable emotion felt from any distance, near and far. The who or what that is loved consumes the mind of the lover.

How are they relative to one another, in one mission of equality to humanity?

The brilliant genius intends to make changes through and with the love of a calling to serve all humanity equally; for all to unite in greater ways of serving each other along with what we have left to salvage for the sake of a planet which the future has lent us.

Stories Told

Through out history man and woman have shared stories to teach their children, their people, and in larger scale-the world. Peering into the world of stories, I contemplate their origins and in theory, conclude that regardless of how realistic or exaggerated they sound…those stories come from either one or many person's experience(s).

Of course those stories evolve as years pass and even though the concerns along with needs of people maintain the basic foundation… invention, industry, and technology challenge these verbal lessons to modernize.

The question I pose is how much of the truth or reality of the original story is lost in the evolution? Is the core of that experience modified to a degree that the one who birthed the account would grieve for the lost message? If we were able to witness or replay the experience, how would we define or separate reality from fantasy in what is shared from one person's view?

In all religions stories are told of epic generational experiences and miracles; of only now to be imagined are embraced and adopted as a way of life. So, what is it that differentiates these stories in defining what becomes dogma, a fairy tale, legend, or folk lore? Why is one a story of miracles and another just story of fluff; even when they both produce the same level of inspiration or motivation?

Now, deeper. Is it impossible for us to interpret a story told by our Earth brothers and sisters (animals) as we learn from their life cycles in observations? Or, is it possible to learn a story from them if we are spiritually connected? What Stories are to be told as we view the emotions of others in passing happiness, sadness, fear, or rejoice? What picture book can we create in a journey of landscapes through not only travels...but in our hearts?

Where does a story begin for you?

Story Teller copy right 2006
Velez Gallery Colorado Springs, CO

Definition vs Intention

Should we always assume that what is meant by ALL people is what has been historically imposed, or, consider that there is always bad and good in all words depending on the intention? Take a look and draw your own conclusion…

Boy defined in dictionary-

noun

1. a youthful male person; "the baby was a boy"; "she made the boy brush his teeth every night"; "most soldiers are only boys in uniform" [syn: <u>male child</u>] [ant: <u>female child</u>]

2. a friendly informal reference to a grown man; "he likes to play golf with the boys"

3. a male human offspring; "their son became a famous judge"; "his boy is taller than he is" [syn: <u>son</u>] [ant: <u>daughter</u>]

4. (ethnic slur) offensive and disparaging term for Black man; "get out of my way, boy"

The 4th definition is how one culture may interpret this one word as offensive or intolerable. Yet in another culture it may be applied as a term of endearment regardless of age. What is your position?

Woman defined in dictionary:

n. pl. wom·en (wĭm'ĭn)

1. An adult female human.

2. Women considered as a group; womankind: "Woman feels the invidious distinctions of sex exactly as the black man does those of color" (Elizabeth Cady Stanton).

3. An adult female human belonging to a specified occupation, group, nationality, or other category. Often used in combination: an Englishwoman; congresswoman; a saleswoman.

4. Feminine quality or aspect; womanliness.

5. A female servant or subordinate.

6. Informal

    a. A wife.

    b. A female lover or sweetheart. See Usage Notes at <u>lady</u>, <u>man</u>, <u>person</u>.

Again, here is another word potentially interpreted as an insult to some... and symbolic as a stage of development for another. What is your view with this word and its various definitions?

Now, is the word ***boy*** more or less acceptable than ***woman*** based on gender? And/or, are the emphasis more prominent according to how each culture perceives them?

When engaging in conversations, do you consider various definitions of words? Before drawing conclusions, do you observe the intention of what message the other person is trying to convey? How can we all improve communication with more awareness of such concepts?

Society

A society ignores a cycle of violence and destruction, never pointing at them-selves.

Who is society? Is it the participants, or the sufferers of crime? Is it the immune class which perpetrators and victims observe from a distance? Or, are you and I society?

What is your society? Is it a group based on ethnicity, belief, or tradition? Or, is it all of us as a group attempting to survive and live together with minimal struggles?

Do you choose your society? How do you choose your society? What do you require of your society?

Does your society promote, encourage, and inspire you? Or does your society enable you with excuses for poor choices, actions, and annihilation of yourselves?

What part of your society are you? Are you a leader or protector...and do you share, empower, or demonstrate solutions to better futures? Or, are you one *society* calls "you people" or "a statistic".

Do you define what society is to you? Or, do you follow the definitions a society imposes on all?

> I think our role in society is what we make it. A lot of times we feel a certain predisposition to labels placed on us by society and we limit ourselves to those labels.
>
> Al
>
> SEPTEMBER 3, 2008 9:03 AM

Is it our responsibility to change society's perception of us? How/what do we change society in a way that benefits community?

Marissa

SEPTEMBER 10, 2008 8:16 AM

Yes, it is our responsibility to change society's perception of us. Now whether or not an individual is complacent with their social label is another story. But I think the best way to improve our society is through a concept called "cultural grounding". I read about this concept in an article by Dr. Maulana Karenga I read for my Afro-American Studies class. From my understanding, "cultural grounding" is the education and growth of an individual being applied throughout his life in efforts to better his self and those around him. I think that if we all practiced a little "cultural grounding", the world would have no choice but to prosper.

Al

SEPTEMBER 10, 2008 9:31 AM

A cult a cliché with color coded ignorance, vigorously blended into an ideal systemized genocide. When thinking outside of the box, ones ethnicity will always emerge. But, when confined to an environment with disbelief how can those that are blinded seem to relinquish their every incarceration. William

OCTOBER 1, 2008 11:31 AM

Sankofa-Blog III

Silent Voice, Prevailing Pen

She sits atop a white truck camper watching traffic on the free way pass, while the train on the other side moves with steady clanking. The sun is warm and the breeze is cool.

Earlier in the morning she is mocked by a family member and the way she speaks becomes a target for cruel laughter-and has been since she can remember. She says not another word but, finds one of her places of escape from the gradual damage it inflicts upon her self-esteem and confidence. Within time she becomes self conscious and only talks with selected friends and her Father. As she begins to emerge from childhood methods of analyzing events, people, and life-loneliness continues to grow for fear of expressing her curiosity, thoughts, and theories in what she is convinced that all others hear as inadequate speech. It is not just the speech. But, it is also the content which she longs to discuss. Fear. Fear of getting in trouble, being judged, or labeled by her parents of two preceding generations. She cares not for any additional negative attention.

Her interest in books ignites a safe place for her voice to be heard. She thinks, "I too can write. And, there is nothing to suffer in pouring the clutter in my mind bleeding through the ink-absorbed by paper." With pen in hand, she begins with a half filled homework binder. For the first time, ever, the girl is freed from stifling fear, seclusion, and gagged thoughts. The binders begin to take on life...her life. She doesn't hide them, but places them in a safe desk drawer. To her new found passion she adds pens for a variety for designing letters and symbols; pencils for sketches of illustrations to complete the entries. She discovers her short pieces in the form of home made gift cards and mini posters are accepted and praised by who she gifts them with.

She chooses not to share the note book journals and for some naive reason, there is a strong belief that no one will violate their sacred place. Then comes the test. On a brisk refreshing autumn afternoon she is walking her dog home from the hills of yuccas and larking birds. Another family member approaches her with what appears to be one of her journals. Her throat tightens up and she grips the leash handle with white knuckles; anticipating the first devastating blow to yet another form of how she expresses herself. The woman holds the journal out before the twelve year old girl who has been writing in a mental state of peace and bliss for the last two years. The woman begins to scold the girl "You need to stop writing this foolishness! It doesn't make sense! What are you thinking? No one will ever understand this!" Along with the hurtful words the girl stands speechless as the pages are ripped out of the book, only to be tossed into the wind and carried away with dry colorful leaves. No words can describe the loss of dreams she goes through. Violated. Devastated. Pure anguish salted with deep sadness.

Twenty five years since then have passed. The girl is now an adult and a mother, encouraging her own to fight for their right to be what they choose for the greater good of all. She uses the journals which she chose to never stop writing; as reference for parables of life and to inspire others. She prevailed. She defied. She speaks aloud with a voice of strength and twenty five years worth of journals are breaking out of the boxes they slept in. Today, and all tomorrows, her pen will write on the hearts of others with hope, love, and the intent to empower them with the same faith in themselves.

If chosen, in the hand of each individual, is grasped the most powerful tool in existence-written word. Every person born, and yet to be born has a story to tell. For the thousands of publications in existence is ten fold the voices contained within their pages. Recordings and testaments of travel, discovery, invention, events, and even what may have been considered just a simple thought of its time; echoes toward us with messages to learn and excel from. Both good and bad coexist as demonstrated in what we read about atrocities, in contrast to victories of the human race. Turn to authors of the past who unveiled truths of their people, experiences unimaginable, and how they gave both a voice for us to learn from. Without the source of written word to return to, where would we be...and how would it affect cultures and who they are? With words only carried in the wind, would awareness or knowledge of what came to pass be as prevalent? True that actions speak louder than words... in most cases the first solid action is writing the intention, to be followed by remaining committed to your written word. We all have the power to write better endings-and chapters full of peace, love, and world changing content. What is your story... and when you share it, what will it contribute to what is more important than to you alone? Mean it and write it... write it and mean it!

I have included the following links with the purpose of additional resources. With the awareness that students attending this class may vary in cultures, ethnicity, and heritage please view this opportunity to explore African American Studies for what it is-being educated on the history of a people who have had a great influence and impact on what our country is today. All cultures and their contributions are of crucial importance to Northern America; thus let this learning experience encourage us to explore the others with what written words have been left behind; to discover our similarities and differences as a means to grow together in this wondrous world of life through literature.

African American Writers:

Wikipedia-
http://en.wikipedia.org/wiki/African_American_literature

19th Century Female Writers-
http://digital.nypl.org/schomburg/writers_aa19/toc.html

Celebrating African American Writers-
http://frank.mtsu.edu/~vvesper/afam.html

Additional Resources:

Origins of African American Literature-
http://books.google.com/books?id=lNFxok6gBD0C&printsec=frontc
over&dq=african+american+authors

African American Literature Book Club-
http://aalbc.com/

Writing Black-
http://www.keele.ac.uk/depts/as/Literature/amlit-black.html

Black Books Direct-
http://www.blackbooksdirect.com/

As I read this entry, I felt like I was reading about myself. I have many of the issues that the young lady has in the entry because I am a person that is afraid of being hurt, I am a person that has very low self esteem, and I am a person of very little words until I have time to sit down and think to myself. I compare myself to the young lady because when I was younger I began to write because I did not have anybody to talk to. But, even though I can compare myself to her as I have grown to become a woman I have told myself that when my son gets older I want to be the one who will listens to him and when he doesn't have the confidence to stand up for himself, I want to be there to tell him you can do it and I want to be the rock for him that I wish I had.

Cyndi

NOVEMBER 24, 2008 4:46 PM

Cyndi,

I share the same sentiments as a mother.

We are the core of our sons' and daughters' praise-leading to their achievements. Through the laughter, tears, defeat, and triumph they will inevitably encounter... the stone, the pillar, and the strength they lean upon- we are, from the moment of babes opening eyes to the milestone of all graduations. Yes, we say to them, "I believe in you".

Thank you for sharing this, and all of your intriguing views in each post. Excellent work and keep leading your son from the front.

Marissa

NOVEMBER 24, 2008 7:19 PM

Being strong and confident is something that is hard for African Americans do- especially on their own or when they don't have the support that they need from home. Children with disabilities have it even worse. As we learned in my African American Studies class there are many different types of black art. Writing is a great way to express your voice and I am pleased to see that even with her disability she kept her own voice and pasted down that belief to her children. I think that this is a great example for everyone to teach to their children and themselves.

Angel

NOVEMBER 25, 2008 4:06 PM

Angel,

Indeed, love is the home and family is the foundation. Regardless of the family structure or lack of, the support begins there and continues on through the following generations.

Each of us encounters the challenges of life... even within the reflection we see every morning. Some have self defeating thoughts "I am not smart enough, rich enough, skilled, etc." It comes down to being the adult of the here and now, holding on to our dreams, and making every day great...or not. The choice is ours. Each difficulty we face is only temporary and one more burden out of the way, making room for all of the better days to come.

We lead children of the future from the front and Angel; I think you'll do a fine job by starting here and recognizing one of the first steps to multiplying that success.

Great work and thank you!

Marissa

NOVEMBER 25, 2008 4:31 PM

I read this story and I see not only myself in this story but, many people out there in this world I believe are afraid. I believe in our life we have felt alone for example when I decided to go back to school I felt I was all alone. I am finding out that I am far from being alone in my quest for education at a non- traditional age. As a result to my experience I encourage everyone I know if they want that higher education they should definitely go for it no matter what others may think!!!!

Sherry

NOVEMBER 25, 2008 7:56 PM

Marissa said...

Sherry~

Try this one:

Significant Others on the Spectrums Blog

It is your destiny to sculpt :)

Marissa

NOVEMBER 25, 2008 8:05 PM

Syncopation

Syncopation of cultures in a rhythm of Earth's heart beat. We hear the harmonies that cause us to express emotions that cannot be laid in words. Notes in a voice, instrument, and score call us forth to join in dance, movement, and joy. We long for the contentment which is brought to us from this force which disappears at birth, and is not tangible through other synesthesia used to experience all else surrounding us. Just to be near the fulfillment of the tune we whistle, hum, tap, and snap without the prerequisite of being an intellectual-for if we turn to the primitive melodies of our ancestors, all that was required was an appreciation for the dance it stirred in our very being. Now, it is the modern path of pain, happiness, anger, and sometimes bliss through which we transmit and broadcast a personal truth and testimony of our own life. Classical, Reggae, R&B, Blues, Jazz, Rock and Roll, and all of the endless genres that continue to multiply new categories; in each is a song to suit the life of one or many. Fathers and Mothers of our past, the great gift you sent down to us for sake of celebrations, traditions, and culture-we continue the production of an art, with the purpose of composers inviting us into their language of life-and the effect causing us to exalt into motion of its call.

copy right 2007

Rhythm causes different emotions in our lives' and we can relate to these different sounds and soon come to appreciate and relate to the different forms of sounds that are produced from instruments and through voices. We live our lives' day by day with a constant flow of rhythm and we never pay attention to it, but I feel that I live my life with a beat in my heart that keeps me motivated and keeps me inspired to live and move further.

Cyndi

NOVEMBER 24, 2008 5:08 PM

Syncopation is about different types of cultures where they don't know how to express themselves by writing it down. So they express themselves differently by using music, poetry, or through something that they love. Also in the blog it stated that the different cultures recognized dance movements and joy to express how they feel. I intend to agree because in my African American culture we tend to express ourselves through reap song or poetry so we can relate to others.

Paul

NOVEMBER 25, 2008 6:35 PM

Symbolic Art

Before written word, indigenous peoples created the means to communicate legends, stories, and events through symbols. Within the eye of what we see in authentic ancestral art, is much more than what is to be perceived as enticing visual pleasure and carvings or paintings of curiosity. The art seen in sculptures, masks, and other indigenous pieces is a reminder to its people of principles, moral values, and the foundation from which its society succeeds in unification; through beliefs and upheld standards of pride in tradition.

Imagine what indigenous ethnic groups would experience, upon viewing their symbols in our interior design, clothing, and other aesthetic fashions. They would view their form of communication as an evolved medium of art.

Traveling along the time line of art, we observe the same evolution as demonstrated by some of our greatest masters still conveying messages; inspiring architecture, writing, and inspiring emotion to continue the mission of creativity.

Art is the desire of a man to express himself, to record the reactions of his personality to the world he lives in. ~Amy Lowell

Symbols copyright 2007

Symbols:

History of a symbol- http://www.collectorsguide.com/fa/fa086.shtml

Meaning of Chicago's flag- http://www.chicagopostcardmuseum.org/meaning_of_the_chicago_flag.html

Petroglyphs- http://www.lonker.net/art_aboriginal_1.htm

http://www.lonker.net/art_african_1.htm

State Your Claim

Weekend has passed and all the ladies went shopping. A red top, a
few styles of shoes, and others with the
latest up-does.

All that fashion, thinking it's aimed toward passion.
Wait! Why do women indulge in this frenzy of colors,
body modification, and cat walk stratification?

Take a closer look at the lie we learned-taught that
trends and beauty is how everything is earned.

A method, if you will-recognize the purpose this
imposition serves not us, but how we are kept. After
a day in un-natural heels and critiques you could have
wept.

What's worse is the division among us this parade
creates. The popular, superior, and smug behavior
it demonstrates.

Face it! We don't do it to impress the men, get the
position, or even for ourselves. It's a dance of competition,
imitating birds, fairies, and elves.

It doesn't improve our intellect, what we learn, or how
we contribute to a better world. It does strip us of our
sisterhood and dreams you had as a little girl.

There's an ancient belief of where we fit in and how we are
tucked away. Supporting and encouraging each other is the
answer to how we defy that today.

Surpass the fads, colors, race, and faiths-be sisters again and defeat
the suppressing wraiths.

Nourish your minds, enhance your lives, compete no more and
flourish in every stride.

The next time you judge one another in that doubtful voice, contemplate and ask "Isn't there a better way and what are the results base on my choice?"

Mothers, daughters, sisters, aunts, and friends...we all have a duty, a vision, and a name...isn't it time to state our claim?

360

A circle, a symbol. Things that have passed, are, and will come to be. Traditions, cultures, creation, and inventions all revolving around like the shape. All things leaving to return in a cycle.

Love, an emotion and an action. Moving through us all; covering the sphere we call earth. Soothing the woes, bringing about smiles, and inspiring the will to do good. Transcending race, religion, and man created bias. A noun and verb given, multiplying, and returning.

According to some studies, the circle was divided into 360 degrees 4,400 years ago to track the passage of the sun, planets, and stars. It is the shape which we all move within down to the very existence of our microscopic being . Love too is endlessly defined in the same pattern, traced as the one connection between us in an ongoing cycle. Place them together and discover what most miss in a relationship.

Imagine you and the one you love in the center of a circle. At the starting point is passionate desire, excitement, and a thirst to know every little detail about that one person. Travel the line and things appear to take a new turn on the rail of life. You both develop a more practical sense of things with all of the exteriors like work, money, bills and responsibility. You begin to notice a few subtle things about the other person that you mentally question; being slightly grazed with a hint of doubt. Once you get past the butterflies and uncertainties, the two of you advance to a new turn and decide that a higher level of commitment is suitable for you both. Work, home, and personal time seem as though they are merging into one. More outside challenges bleed into the circle and stress is taking on its own character. You are nearing the end of a cycle and now the two of you no longer do the special little things that created a healthy and joyful bond between you both. Just one more turn and you have the ability to start a new circle with two options.

You can keep repeating where you are and know where you are headed. Or, you can rekindle the starting point, adding new acts of love to the experiences you share. With this replenishment you have an awareness that all of the exterior distraction will always be there and the two of you can find ways to over come them. You will not always have the same interests. Yet you can have a mutual respect for each other; and honor that through those interests the other person feels joy and enriches their spirit. Find new ways to demonstrate a healthy and "round about" ways to act out your love toward that person. Know that there cannot be good without bad, happy without sad, and that your loved one has the right to every emotion they encounter. Never assume they know what's on your mind or you know what's one theirs. Consistently communicate with honesty and sincerity even when you agree to disagree. Treat each other as each day is your last. Be creative and find unique ways to tell him/her you love them. Do not allow the negativity of outside influences inside your circle of love; the communication between you is not to be substituted by the assumptions and opinions of others. Live out loud together in laughter, dance, song, and making effort to experience something new each day. Believe and have faith in one another's dreams, vision, and efforts to fulfill them.

More simply put, secure your circle of love in all 360 degree angles by making all 365 days of each year worth a life time poem of two becoming and remaining one. The math behind it all:

For each 360 days in a year, demonstrate your love for him/her in a new way.

For each of the remaining 5 days, celebrate each other and reflect on what made your bond stronger. Hmm... Does this mean five more angles and a bigger circle to soar in? Be creative and you decide!

Love and Fear copyright 2006

"360" life , death where we came from, were we go, who we know, are in the personal circle. Then we add a wife/husband and a child, or two. Your circle gets bigger every day, ever year. Some were at the start of the circle who find out your skin color may try to stop you from dreaming big. If you stop a dream in the beginning you have no chance to have a full circle. This is what's stopping some of are youth.

K

NOVEMBER 22, 2008 6:15 PM

K,

Work from the end where you see your dream, walk by faith and transcend what others see, the youth will see you and follow to the same cycle in their own vision.

Easier said than done, but, attainable when you simply believe in your calling. DREAM BIG!!!

Marissa

NOVEMBER 24, 2008 7:32 PM

This blog entry is very nice because people that are in relationships don't take time out to realize and to understand that things don't always go right, but people must remember that we are all individuals and we are not going to agree all the time, but we need to be able to compromise and work together to make things better. This can be very helpful to some because there may be someone out there that is having relationship problems and they might be ready to give up but this may help them to work out the problem and figure out some solutions. People look at relationships and take them too lightly because I personally never has sat down and thought about the days like that and maybe if we as individuals do that things may be better in the long run.

Cyndi W.

NOVEMBER 24, 2008 5:02 PM

This blog is about people who are in a relationship; who need to understand that in a relationship you have to understand each other and know that you will not always see eye too eye. This lets you know that every relationship will not be perfect. You need to know it cannot be good without the bad. You need to always communicate and have honesty; do not allow negative energy to hurt you.

NOVEMBER 25, 2008 6:43 PM

This blog is about relationships and how you do what you have to do. Either stay together or just move on. Every relationship is not always going to be the same as everyone else's. There is always someone to help with relationship problems. The little things can get bigger and bigger by the second.

Paul

NOVEMBER 25, 2008 7:28 PM

I see this blog as explaining love and how it evolves just like people and the earth. Love is a tricky emotion that can sometimes be confused with lust. When you have love for someone things around you become so much more valuable throughout the cycle of love. Love is a very strong emotion and feeling that reoccurs throughout the cycle of love. Love symbolizes great things and doesn't discriminate against just as the sun doesn't.

Angel

NOVEMBER 25, 2008 11:43 PM

I, the Ghetto

With me, what you see is what you get. I am very generous in the manner which I do not discriminate. You may have seen me in the projects or in the eyes of a slum lord. I keep my people neatly tucked away even though there isn't any form of unity in their community. They are all in survival mode and the cost they pay to do so is much higher than what's observed on the surface of a cold reality. See, I work very hard through the efforts of others' greed, prejudice, and power starved motivations. Let me walk you through the stages of my development in an individual; then how I am multiplied through others.

A pregnant woman has just returned home from a double shift. Feet burn, back is tight with pain. The worse part is her hunger that is doubled with the life in her belly. Two more days till a pay check is in hand. The lights dim out of her control and she fails to restore them with a switch on the wall. No power except mine-and you can't cook with that! She grabs the remains of stale crackers, a cup of water, and consumes them to the sound of a grumbling stomach, a fetus kicking, and her tears to flavor the water.

You may be thinking that I begin with her. But, that's not the case since she is an adult and she is already a part of my people. No challenge there...she has submitted to the life of my world and would never contemplate making a change with her neighbors, or, alone for that matter. I have begun my influence on her child within. He senses her transgression, shares the hunger, and possibly uncertain health upon birth. This nine month training transitions into the moment of the first contraction she experiences walking home late at night.

Soon after she is at a registration desk in the hospital where she is treated like a number due to being a statistic of the system. The questions come as a rushing river where her emotions are washed into a pitfall of darkness, "Don't you know where the father is? What is his name? What is your case worker's number?" The episode continues into the labor room where my new apprentice greets the world with lungs and voice of what could make him the next great leader, humanitarian, or what ever he chooses through the free will bestowed upon all men and women.

Mama continues to work and now half her pay check goes to child care; and constant visits to the doctor for ear infections, colds, and other ailments. The land lord won't fix the leaking toilet or the faulty heating system. Mama wants to return to school but, she discovers the educational programs dictate her profession; still locking her into being one of my people. She tries anyway. My little apprentice soon moves onto preschool and is exposed to the reinforced life I impose, shared by other children of his economic like. Some nice, some violent, others with special needs not receiving services. The playground is sometimes a dumpsite for needles and used contraceptives. The teachers try their best to keep the children safe and tend to their learning through what little income is earned and what minimal funding is provided for the class room.

Little man moves on into following grades where he may have to fight to keep his winter coat donated. If there is one thing I want my children to know, is that they must take from each other, at any cost to get what they want and keep what they have. Being a united force for a better world is against my policies and keeps the politics of it all as my greatest ally. It is I who whispers into the ears of the wealthy and privileged-that there is not enough to go around so we must keep my people in my presence of the ongoing cycle of poverty and struggle.

Little man is confronted with street life, tempted with the quick fix and dollar of hustling, and no father to mentor him into his right of being one of the few who escape my generous tragedy. He's making the grades and doing well till I finally take Mama down with the stress of loosing their home and all that's in it. I made her heart race into the emergency room and now, what's a sixteen year old to do? He loves his mother and can't let her down. She has made sacrifices for him all of his life. So I send him an invitation to hit the street for the all mighty dollar and he becomes one of my fastest and efficient learners. Not only does he catch Mama up on rent, but he now has the clothes and a car worth more than the home they live in.

Mama looks out the window and sees her son on the street-some days talking to the pretty ladies, protecting his corner, and providing a deadly product. She recognizes the defeat in her only child. What can tears season this time? It's the same man made life that was designed to hold her in my arms and to pass it onto him. Now, will his free will conquer my purpose to a society? Probably not. Don't worry though...next year, his child conceived in teen sex can try escaping too. Remember, I do not discriminate. I grow in all environments-apartments, houses, modular homes, and more. You being human alone is enough reason for me to share misery with you...culture, heritage, gender, religion mean nothing to me. I am not the exclusive type. Shun your neighbor, forget parenting, kill your fellow kind, destroy your community and you are all mine. Ah yes, you can move too. I'll catch you in my other "higher" class terrains. Welcome people...glad you live in me...the Ghetto.

For I am grateful that this situation I choose to call Ghetto life is only temporary. My path may have been mapped out when I chose to come into this plane we humans call Earth. But there are infinite possibilities to my mapped out existence, I only have to manifest and make real what one or ones will be yet another chapter in my life!

Love ya soul sista, thank you for indulging me with a tear to my cheek and heart.

Star

SEPTEMBER 11, 2008 9:41 PM

Ghetto is a label or title...actions speak louder than both. Your success is already there...it only has to materialize. Fear not and walk by faith. The old path has been driven, now you soar to unimaginable heights and discover pages in which YOU tell the story :*)

Marissa

SEPTEMBER 11, 2008 11:35 PM

Life in the ghetto is like any other place on earth; you make it the best as you can. The American inner cities ghetto can break down the strongest person. When hope is no were to be found, I think of the ghettos of the world. Just the other day I was talking to a man who up grew up in the Middle East. As a kid he sometime woke to rocket attacks.

Kevin

NOVEMBER 22, 2008 8:00 PM

We go through hard times but as we struggle and fight for the better things in life, how is it that our children always have to end up in the same situations we have gone though even though we have done everything in our power to make them be better than we were?

NOVEMBER 24, 2008 5:20 PM

I liked this one because it's telling how the story goes for most youth born into bad situations. And they are helpless for the most part to change it. It's like we have become so accustomed to trying our best to get out the situation that we sometimes step on others or try to drag others down or just don't end up caring. You see so many people around you messed up it's kinda like you pick up on the things you see and just adapt to the rest.

Shawn

NOVEMBER 25, 2008 12:26 PM

The title of this blog expresses how the community doesn't unite to teach one another or how to help one each other learn. This blog is a metaphor for how the "person" known as the ghetto is perceived and looked at. It kind of tells you one side of a story rather than perception from both sides. The "ghetto" is just a term used to describe it but you can never understand it if you don't see or live it.

Angel

NOVEMBER 25, 2008 5:50 PM

Words...

a powerful tool. We can allow others to control us with them along with fear... or we can absorb a verbiage power to rise above the ill intentions of others. Words can be what we make them but, are most effective when doing what's right and just...with intelligence, humility, and integrity.

Very moving comments Star, Kevin, and Angel

Marissa

NOVEMBER 25, 2008 8:15 PM

Educational Glance

Educational Glance

I endorse and promote education for all individuals. Education provides us with an awareness, appreciation, and power of knowledge to work together for common interests and goals. For most, learning is another milestone in life-symbolic of earning something greater through personal merit and diligence. Then, for others, it is a means to be accepted into certain social classes based more on what they have learned from only text books; and not from the experiences and emotional intelligence of life, proven to be more essential.

From the beginning of our education, we comply with the understanding that we will learn from text books compiled from one society's perspective of our history, philosophy, and how we are to apply its functionality to a way of life. Also, we are taught that if we learn from the same materials, but in different educational establishments... somehow, the learning materials are of higher quality-depending on the name, funding, or location of the school.

Formal education is also generally based on three contributing factors of a career in how or what we choose to pursue. The first of the three is usually based on what society imposes with the concept of what an acceptable income is; according to economics, worthy titles, and prestige within various corporations. Second, an individual may simply choose a profession due to necessity of immediate income-leading to short term education or certificates; supplementing four or more year degree providing limited or no options to advance in finances or in the matrix of a company. Last, are a people who have a strong efficacy and desire to follow a calling of life's work, regardless of the income earned-targeting the career best suiting their needs and contentment, fulfilled with whatever level of learning is required to complete a vision.

I feel that it is important to emphasize that regardless of the amount of class hours earned toward a career, what is more crucial to the success of any professional is the experience surrounding the community which is worked in or served. This is where the true education begins, as what has been learned in a class room, is applied to real life situations. This is the moment when the function of the education is set into motion; and the results of expertise or knowledge of concepts is demonstrated through efficiency of accurately completed tasks and/or endeavors. Learning within the four walls of an institution is not the main source of the function of what we learn; but is the foundation of what and how we achieve by developing into eager learners and scholars. The full circle of continual knowledge truly begins once the foundation is laid and we work together to invent, create, and serve society for an effective and harmonious future.

- How is that sufficient future launched?

- What do we need to improve education in our country as an all inclusive piece to life?

- What components/approaches to learning to we need to omit and/or improve to ensure equality in education?

- What can we learn from other countries and cultures to improve mutual respect for all individuals in all fields of work and research, regardless of where they graduate from?

- Is there a forgotten key found in historical educational methodologies that can open doors to higher quality learning-to bring back the more personal and humanistic side to how we provide services and programs to society (beside manners, customer service, person to person communication opposed to automated phone services, etc.)?

- Should it be a requirement for professionals to learn emotional intelligences in addition to academics to enhance the functionality of education?

These are questions I contemplate upon observing what I would like to see more/less of from educators and within institutions I attend as a student. Please share your ideas and views. Remember, there is no right or wrong answers...only individuals learning from one another to improve the road we pave to a more pleasant future.

> Education is the key to life. Education is knowledge and knowledge is POWER. Education is relevant to our community. Meaning take back what we learn and apply it to where we came from. I must agree with the young lady that said Education is LIFE itself.
>
> Trina
>
> SEPTEMBER 23, 2008 7:43 PM

> Education to me means survival. Without some kind of education (knowledge) of something you can't get very far in life. With an education you can try to decide what you want out of life and from life. It is up to you to go after it. It's very important to have an education because people that don't are getting left behind.
>
> Sinda
>
> SEPTEMBER 24, 2008 6:11 PM

Very compelling Cyndi...

my question for you is, "Are we too focused on the education of ever changing technology, to the degree that we would not know how to survive as a specie without it? Are we relinquishing the core values of humanistic beings by relying so dependently on the automation of the world?

Just a thought :)

Marissa

SEPTEMBER 27, 2008 11:35 AM

Education provides us with an awareness, appreciation, and power of knowledge to work together for common interests and goals. Without in education it becomes hard to communicate with the world.

Sherry

SEPTEMBER 29, 2008 12:16 PM

Education and communication appear to be partnered in your post Shamika. This is an important observation for us all to make-for we may continuously learn what we live... and it would be of no value if we do not apply what we learn to life and share it with others to benefit and create a harmonious society, serving all. Thank you for sharing!

Think like a wise man but communicate in the language of the people.

~William Butler Yeats

Marissa

OCTOBER 13, 2008 9:43 AM

This is challenging the value of a formal education. I agree that all the old textbooks we are learning from are filled with bias. I know we need it to get through school but I don't think we should go by everything we read in there as the 100 percent truth. Like it said we should get most of our learning from life experiences.

Shawn

NOVEMBER 25, 2008 12:34 PM

I think this is a wonderful entry education is the key to everything. getting your education u have completed a mile stone this is the most important thing u need to do with your life, without this u can't make it any where cause u have nothing to fall back on. You can't become anything in life if you do not know anything. I realize how important it was when you only have a high school diploma; that is nothing when you really want to be something. Education is the key.

Katrina

NOVEMBER 25, 2008 6:59 PM

Education is apart of every individuals life. I believe that only learning what's in your textbook won't expand your education. Reading and learning what schools teach you is fine but there is always more than one side to the story. Researching things that you learn for yourself can give you the upper hand of knowing more and being able to make your own conclusions about what you learned. You may have to remember and learn what they teach you in school but you don't have to believe in it.

Angel

NOVEMBER 25, 2008 11:31 PM

The online blogs are a valuable resource with additional links to educational material.

To view my internet blogs along with contributions made by students and professionals, please follow this link to my profile:
www.blogger.com/profile/07807844008273244183

Marissa's online photography and painting gallery:
www.yessy.com/4mymstudio

Please feel free to contact me to arrange custom designed blogs suiting for supplements to academic materials, work shops, leadership/cultural diversity training, etc.

Blog services- mymwrite@gmail.com

Educational resource connection- marissam@q.com